# HOW TO DESIGN YOUR LIFE

## *HOW TO BUILD A WELL-LIVED, JOYFUL LIFE, A FORMAT OF HAPPINESS*

# INTRODUCTION

Have you ever felt like you're stuck in a rut? Like you're just going through the motions of life without any real sense of purpose or joy? If so, you're not alone. Many people feel unfulfilled and dissatisfied with their lives, but the good news is that you don't have to settle for a mediocre existence. You have the power to design your life and create a well-lived, joyful existence.

In this book, I'll guide you through a step-by-step process for designing your life. We'll start by assessing your current situation and identifying what's working and what's not. Then, we'll move on to creating a vision for your ideal life and setting goals that align with your values and purpose. We'll also explore strategies for building healthy habits, creating a supportive environment, navigating challenges and setbacks, cultivating meaningful relationships, pursuing your passions and purpose, and living a balanced life.

But why is designing your life important in the first place? Here are a few reasons:

You'll have more control over your life. When you intentionally design your life, you're taking control of your future. You're not just letting life happen to you, but rather, you're actively shaping it in a way that aligns with your values and goals.

You'll be more fulfilled and satisfied. When you design your life around what's important to you, you're more likely to feel a sense of purpose and meaning. You'll also be more likely to experience positive emotions like joy and contentment.

You'll be better equipped to handle challenges. Life is full of ups and downs, but when you've designed your life intentionally, you'll be better equipped to handle the challenges that come your way. You'll have a sense of direction and purpose that can help you navigate even the toughest situations.

Throughout this book, I'll share practical tips and exercises to help you design your life in a way that brings you joy and fulfillment. Whether you're feeling lost and uncertain, or simply want to make some positive changes in your life, this book will provide you with the tools and guidance you need to create a life you love.

# CHAPTER 1: ASSESSING YOUR CURRENT LIFE

Before you can start designing your ideal life, it's important to assess where you're at right now. This will help you identify what's working and what's not, as well as what changes you might want to make. Here are a few things you can do to assess your current life:

# IDENTIFYING YOUR VALUES, STRENGTHS, AND WEAKNESSES

Your values, strengths, and weaknesses are three important factors that shape your life. By identifying these factors, you'll be able to understand yourself better and make informed decisions that are aligned with who you are.

Values: Your values are the guiding principles that drive your behavior and decisions. They are the things that matter most to you in life, and they can help you prioritize your time and energy. Examples of values include family, health, personal growth, creativity, spirituality, and adventure. To identify your values, start by asking yourself what's most important to you. What do you care about deeply? What motivates you? What makes you feel fulfilled? Make a list of your top 5-10 values and then reflect on how you can live in alignment with them.

Strengths: Your strengths are the things that come naturally to you and that you excel at. They are the skills and qualities that make you unique and valuable. Examples of strengths include creativity, leadership, communication, problem-solving, and empathy. To identify your strengths, ask yourself what you're good at and what comes easily to you. You can also ask friends and family for feedback on what they think your strengths are.

Weaknesses: Your weaknesses are areas where you might struggle or where you don't feel as confident. They are not necessarily bad things, but they can hinder your progress if you don't address them. Examples of weaknesses include procrastination, self-doubt, poor time management, and lack of assertiveness. To identify your weaknesses, reflect on areas where you tend to struggle or where you wish you could improve. You can also ask for feedback from others on areas where they think you could improve.

# ASSESSING YOUR CURRENT LEVEL OF SATISFACTION

To design your ideal life, it's important to understand where you're starting from. Assessing your current level of satisfaction with different areas of your life can help you identify what's working well and what needs improvement.

Take some time to reflect on how satisfied you are with different areas of your life, such as your career, relationships, health, hobbies, spirituality, and anything else that's important to you. Rate your level of satisfaction on a scale from 1-10, and then ask yourself what specifically is contributing to that level of satisfaction (or dissatisfaction). For example, if you rate your career satisfaction as a 6, you might reflect on what aspects of your job are contributing to that rating. Is it the work itself, the people you work with, the salary, or something else?

# REFLECTING ON WHAT YOU WANT MORE (AND LESS) OF IN YOUR LIFE

Based on your values and current level of satisfaction, reflect on what you want more (and less) of in your life. This can help you identify your priorities and guide your decision-making process.

Consider what aspects of your life are currently fulfilling and energizing, and what areas feel draining or unfulfilling. Think about what activities or experiences bring you joy and meaning, and what you wish you had more time for. This reflection can help you identify what you want to prioritize in your life moving forward.

By taking the time to assess your current life, you'll have a clearer sense of what you want to change and what you want to maintain. This will lay the groundwork for the next steps in the design process. In the next chapter, we'll explore how to use your assessments to set goals and create a vision for your ideal life. By understanding where you're starting from, you'll be better equipped to create a plan that's tailored to your unique needs and desires.

# CHAPTER 2: DEFINING YOUR IDEAL LIFE

Once you've assessed your current life, it's time to start defining your ideal life. This involves creating a vision for the future you want to create and setting goals that will help you get there. Here are a few steps you can take to define your ideal life:

# CREATING A VISION FOR YOUR IDEAL LIFE

A vision is a clear and compelling picture of the future you want to create. It's a mental image that inspires and motivates you, and that you can use as a guide for your decision-making. To create a vision for your ideal life, take some time to imagine what your life would look like if everything was exactly the way you wanted it to be. Consider the following questions:

What kind of work would you be doing, and how would it make you feel?

What kind of relationships would you have, and how would they nourish and support you?

What kind of physical and mental health would you have, and how would you take care of yourself?

What kind of hobbies and interests would you pursue, and how would they bring you joy and fulfillment?

What kind of impact would you want to make in the world, and how would you make it happen?

As you answer these questions, try to be as specific and detailed as possible. Use vivid language and create a mental picture that feels real and exciting to you.

# SETTING GOALS THAT ALIGN WITH YOUR VALUES AND VISION

Once you have a clear vision of your ideal life, it's time to start setting goals that will help you get there. Goals are specific, measurable, and time-bound objectives that help you move towards your vision. To set goals that align with your values and vision, consider the following:

☐ Prioritize: Look at your values and vision and identify the most important areas you want to focus on. Set goals that align with these priorities.

☐ Be specific: Make sure your goals are clear and specific. Instead of setting a goal to "exercise more," set a goal to "go for a 30-minute walk three times a week."

☐ Make them measurable: Set goals that you can track and measure. This will help you see your progress and stay motivated. For example, instead of setting a goal to "get better at public speaking," set a goal to "give a 5-minute presentation at a networking event next month."

☐ Make them time-bound: Set a deadline for your goals to give yourself a sense of urgency and motivation. This will help you stay focused and on track.

# CREATING AN ACTION PLAN TO MOVE TOWARDS YOUR GOALS

Once you have your goals, it's important to create an action plan to help you achieve them. An action plan is a specific and detailed plan that outlines the steps you need to take to reach your goals. Here are a few tips for creating an action plan:

- ☐ Break it down: Break your goals down into smaller, manageable tasks. This will make them less overwhelming and easier to tackle.
- ☐ Be specific: Be as specific as possible about what you need to do and when. Create a timeline and a list of action steps for each goal.
- ☐ Anticipate obstacles: Think about what obstacles you might face and how you can overcome them. This will help you stay prepared and motivated.
- ☐ Review regularly: Review your action plan regularly and adjust it as needed. This will help you stay on track and make progress towards your goals.

By creating a clear vision, setting goals that align with your values and vision, and creating an action plan to move towards your goals, you'll be well on your way to designing your ideal life. In the next chapter, we'll explore how to take action and make changes in your life that will help you move towards your vision.

# CHAPTER 3: BUILDING HEALTHY HABITS

Habits are powerful tools for designing your life. They are the small, repeated actions that you take every day that shape your identity and determine your future. Whether you want to improve your health, build better relationships, or advance in your career, building healthy habits is key. In this chapter, we'll explore the importance of habits in designing your life, how to identify and break bad habits, and tips for developing and sustaining good habits.

# THE IMPORTANCE OF HABITS IN DESIGNING YOUR LIFE

Habits are the building blocks of your life. They shape your behavior, influence your decisions, and determine your outcomes. By building healthy habits, you can create a life that is aligned with your values and vision. Here are a few benefits of building healthy habits:

☐ Consistency: Habits create consistency in your life. By doing something repeatedly, you make it a part of your routine and it becomes easier to maintain.

☐ Motivation: Habits help you stay motivated. When you see progress and improvement over time, it can inspire you to keep going.

☐ Discipline: Habits require discipline, which is a valuable skill in all areas of life. By building healthy habits, you can develop your discipline and apply it to other areas of your life.

# IDENTIFYING AND BREAKING BAD HABITS

Before you can build healthy habits, it's important to identify and break bad habits. Bad habits are behaviors that are not aligned with your values and vision, and that hold you back from reaching your goals. Here are a few tips for identifying and breaking bad habits:

- ☐ Be honest with yourself: Admitting that you have a bad habit can be difficult, but it's the first step towards change. Be honest with yourself about the habits that are holding you back.
- ☐ Identify triggers: Bad habits are often triggered by certain situations or emotions. Identify the triggers that lead to your bad habits and find ways to avoid them or manage them.
- ☐ Replace with a good habit: Instead of trying to eliminate a bad habit, replace it with a good one. This will help you create a positive change in your life.

# DEVELOPING AND SUSTAINING GOOD HABITS

Once you've identified and broken bad habits, it's time to start developing and sustaining good habits. Here are a few tips for building healthy habits:

☐ Start small: Focus on one habit at a time and start small. Trying to change too much too quickly can be overwhelming and discouraging.

☐ Be consistent: Consistency is key when it comes to building habits. Aim to do your habit every day, even if it's just for a few minutes.

☐ Use positive reinforcement: Celebrate your successes and give yourself positive reinforcement when you do your habit. This will help you stay motivated and make your habit more enjoyable.

☐ Make it enjoyable: Find ways to make your habit enjoyable. Whether it's listening to music while you exercise or practicing a hobby you love, making your habit enjoyable will help you stick with it.

# TIPS FOR CREATING HEALTHY HABITS THAT STICK

Here are a few additional tips for creating healthy habits that stick:

- ☐ Choose habits that align with your values and vision
- ☐ Make your habit a non-negotiable part of your routine
- ☐ Use reminders to help you stay on track
- ☐ Find an accountability partner to help you stay motivated
- ☐ Track your progress to see how far you've come

By building healthy habits, you can create a life that is aligned with your values and vision. In the next chapter, we'll explore how to cultivate a positive mindset that will help you achieve your goals and overcome obstacles.

# CHAPTER 4: CREATING A SUPPORTIVE ENVIRONMENT

Your environment has a significant impact on your life. It can either support or hinder your ability to design a life that aligns with your values and vision. In this chapter, we'll explore the importance of creating a supportive environment, how to assess your current environment, and tips for making changes to support your goals and well-being.

# THE IMPACT OF YOUR ENVIRONMENT ON YOUR LIFE

Your environment includes your physical surroundings, social networks, and cultural influences. All of these elements can either contribute to or detract from your well-being and ability to achieve your goals. For example, if you live in a cluttered and disorganized home, it may be difficult to focus on your work or relax and unwind. On the other hand, if you surround yourself with supportive friends and family members, they can provide encouragement and motivation to help you achieve your goals.

# ASSESSING YOUR CURRENT ENVIRONMENT

Before you can make changes to your environment, it's important to assess your current situation. Here are a few questions to ask yourself:

How does your physical environment make you feel? Is it cluttered or organized? Is it conducive to productivity and relaxation?
Who are the people in your social network? Are they supportive and positive influences? Do they share your values and vision?
What are the cultural influences in your life? Do they align with your values and vision? Do they inspire you or detract from your well-being?
Making Changes to Your Environment

Once you've assessed your current environment, it's time to make changes to support your goals and well-being. Here are a few tips:

- ☐ Create a vision for your ideal environment: What do you want your physical, social, and cultural environments to look like? How do you want them to make you feel?
- ☐ Make small changes: Making drastic changes to your environment can be overwhelming. Instead, start by making small changes that will have a positive impact on your well-being.
- ☐ Surround yourself with positive influences: Seek out people who share your values and vision, and who will support and encourage you.
- ☐ Eliminate negative influences: If there are people or cultural

influences in your life that detract from your well-being, consider minimizing or eliminating them.

☐   Use your environment as a tool: Your environment can be a powerful tool for achieving your goals. For example, if you want to exercise more, create a workout space in your home that is inviting and motivating.

# CHAPTER 5: NAVIGATING CHALLENGES AND SETBACKS

Designing your life is a process that involves ups and downs, successes and failures. While it's important to have a clear vision for your ideal life and to set achievable goals, it's equally important to prepare for the inevitable challenges and setbacks that you will encounter along the way.

# STRATEGIES FOR DEALING WITH SETBACKS AND FAILURES

Setbacks and failures can be discouraging, but they are a natural part of any journey. In fact, they can be valuable opportunities for growth and learning. However, it's important to have strategies in place to help you deal with setbacks when they arise.

One strategy is to practice self-compassion. It's important to be kind to yourself and acknowledge that setbacks and failures are a part of the learning process. When you experience a setback, try to avoid being overly critical of yourself. Instead, remind yourself that setbacks are common, and that they can be valuable learning opportunities.

Another strategy is to reframe setbacks as opportunities for growth. Instead of seeing setbacks as failures, view them as opportunities to learn and grow. Reflect on what went wrong, and what you can do differently next time. By doing this, you can turn a setback into a valuable learning experience.

# STAYING MOTIVATED AND OVERCOMING OBSTACLES

Staying motivated and overcoming obstacles are essential for designing a well-lived, joyful life. Obstacles can be frustrating and discouraging, but they don't have to derail your progress. Here are some strategies that can help you overcome obstacles and stay motivated:

- ☐ Break goals into smaller, manageable tasks: When faced with a daunting goal, break it down into smaller, more manageable tasks. This can make the goal feel more achievable and help you make steady progress.
- ☐ Use positive self-talk: Instead of focusing on what you can't do, focus on what you can do and use positive self-talk to stay motivated. Encourage yourself and remind yourself of your progress.
- ☐ Stay flexible: Be open to adjusting your approach when faced with obstacles or challenges. If one strategy isn't working, try another approach.
- ☐ Celebrate small wins: Celebrate your progress, even if it's small. This can help you stay motivated and build momentum.

# LEARNING FROM MISTAKES

Mistakes are a natural part of any journey, and they can be valuable opportunities for growth and learning. However, it's important to approach mistakes with a growth mindset. Here are some tips for learning from your mistakes:

- ☐ Reflect on what went wrong: Take the time to reflect on what went wrong and why. Be honest with yourself, but avoid being overly critical or judgmental.
- ☐ Identify what you can do differently: Use what you've learned to identify what you can do differently in the future. This can help you avoid making the same mistake again.
- ☐ Stay positive: Approach mistakes with a growth mindset and use them as opportunities to learn and grow. Remember that mistakes are a natural part of any journey, and that they can help you become a stronger, more resilient person.

By practicing self-compassion, staying focused on your vision, and approaching obstacles with a growth mindset, you can overcome challenges and continue making progress towards your goals. In the next chapter, we'll explore the importance of cultivating meaningful relationships and connections.

# CHAPTER 6: CULTIVATING MEANINGFUL RELATIONSHIPS

Life is about relationships. Whether it's with family, friends, colleagues, or even strangers, our interactions with others have a significant impact on our overall well-being. Strong relationships can provide us with support, happiness, and a sense of purpose. On the other hand, toxic relationships can drain our energy and hinder our personal growth. Therefore, designing a well-lived life requires a conscious effort to cultivate meaningful relationships.

# THE IMPORTANCE OF RELATIONSHIPS IN A WELL-LIVED LIFE

Research has consistently shown that having positive relationships is linked to greater happiness, better physical health, and a longer life. A study conducted by Harvard University found that good relationships are the strongest predictor of a happy life. People who have supportive relationships are less likely to experience stress, depression, and other mental health issues. In contrast, social isolation can be detrimental to our health, with studies indicating that it can be as harmful as smoking and obesity.

# NURTURING EXISTING RELATIONSHIPS

The first step in cultivating meaningful relationships is to nurture the ones that already exist. This involves being present, showing appreciation, and actively listening to others. It's easy to take our loved ones for granted, especially when we're busy with work and other commitments. However, it's essential to make time for the people who matter most in our lives. Simple gestures like sending a text message, having a coffee date, or doing a small favor can go a long way in maintaining strong relationships.

Another crucial aspect of nurturing existing relationships is communication. Good communication skills are essential for building trust, resolving conflicts, and expressing our needs and wants effectively. It's crucial to be honest and transparent with our loved ones, even when it's uncomfortable or challenging. Building a foundation of trust and mutual respect can create a safe space where we can share our vulnerabilities and grow together.

# BUILDING NEW RELATIONSHIPS THAT ALIGN WITH YOUR VALUES AND GOALS

In addition to nurturing existing relationships, designing a well-lived life also involves building new relationships that align with our values and goals. This doesn't mean that we need to go out and make a bunch of new friends or join every social club in town. Instead, it's about being intentional and purposeful about the relationships we pursue.

When we're clear about our values and goals, we're better able to identify the types of people and communities that will support us in achieving them. For example, if we're passionate about environmental issues, joining a local conservation group can connect us with like-minded individuals who share our values. If we're interested in starting a business, attending networking events can help us meet potential partners and mentors who can provide guidance and support.

Cultivating meaningful relationships is an ongoing process that requires effort and intentionality. It's about showing up, being present, and investing in the people who matter most to us. It's also about being open to new experiences and opportunities to connect with others who share our values and goals. By prioritizing relationships, we can create a supportive and fulfilling environment that enriches our lives and contributes to our overall well-being.

# CHAPTER 7: PURSUING YOUR PASSIONS AND PURPOSE

Living a well-lived, joyful life means pursuing your passions and living with purpose. Unfortunately, many people don't know what their passions are, let alone how to turn them into a meaningful career or purpose. In this chapter, we'll explore the importance of passion and purpose, how to identify your passions, and how to make them an integral part of your life.

# THE ROLE OF PASSION AND PURPOSE IN A JOYFUL LIFE

Passion and purpose give your life meaning and direction. Passion is what drives you, motivates you, and fills you with energy and enthusiasm. It's the thing that makes you jump out of bed in the morning, eager to tackle the day ahead. Purpose, on the other hand, is the reason why you do what you do. It's the bigger picture, the long-term goal that gives your life direction and meaning.

# IDENTIFYING YOUR PASSIONS AND PURPOSE

To pursue your passions and live with purpose, you first need to identify what they are. Ask yourself: What do I love to do? What brings me joy and fulfillment? What are my natural talents and strengths? What issues or causes do I care deeply about? Once you have a sense of what your passions are, you can start exploring how to incorporate them into your life.

# MAKING TIME FOR YOUR PASSIONS AND INCORPORATING THEM INTO YOUR LIFE

Many people struggle to find the time to pursue their passions, especially if they have a busy career or family life. But it's essential to make time for the things that bring you joy and fulfillment. Look for ways to incorporate your passions into your daily routine, even if it's just for a few minutes a day. You might also need to make some sacrifices or changes in your life to prioritize your passions.

# USING YOUR PASSIONS AND PURPOSE TO MAKE A POSITIVE IMPACT ON THE WORLD

Your passions and purpose can also be used to make a positive impact on the world. By aligning your passions and purpose with a cause or issue you care about, you can make a meaningful difference in the world. This could be through volunteer work, advocacy, or even starting your own business or non-profit organization.

Pursuing your passions and living with purpose is an essential aspect of designing your life. It gives your life meaning and direction, and allows you to make a positive impact on the world. By identifying your passions and purpose, making time for them, and incorporating them into your life, you can create a life that's not just well-lived, but also joyful and fulfilling.

# CHAPTER 8: LIVING A BALANCED LIFE

In today's fast-paced world, it's easy to get caught up in the demands of work and forget about the other important aspects of life. However, living a well-lived life requires balance. It's about finding harmony between work, play, productivity, relaxation, and everything else that makes life worth living.

# THE IMPORTANCE
# OF BALANCE

When we are out of balance, it's easy to become overwhelmed and stressed. We may struggle to focus, feel unfulfilled, and experience a sense of disconnection from ourselves and others. Conversely, when we achieve balance, we feel more grounded, focused, and at peace.

# BALANCING WORK AND PLAY

Work and play are both essential aspects of a balanced life. However, many of us struggle to find the right balance between the two. We may get so caught up in our work that we forget to make time for the things we enjoy, or we may feel guilty when we take time off.

To achieve balance between work and play, it's important to create clear boundaries. This means setting aside specific times for work and specific times for play, and sticking to them as much as possible. It also means learning to switch off from work when we're not working, so we can fully engage in the things that bring us joy.

# BALANCING PRODUCTIVITY AND RELAXATION

In addition to balancing work and play, it's also essential to find a balance between productivity and relaxation. This means learning to work efficiently when we need to, but also making time for rest and relaxation.

One way to achieve this is by practicing good time management skills. This involves prioritizing our tasks and focusing on the most important things first. It also means learning to delegate tasks when necessary and avoiding procrastination.

When it comes to relaxation, it's important to find activities that help us unwind and recharge. This could be anything from reading a book to taking a walk in nature, or spending time with loved ones. By making relaxation a priority, we can reduce stress and boost our overall well-being.

# CREATING BALANCE IN YOUR LIFE

Finding balance in life is an ongoing process. It requires awareness, intention, and a willingness to make changes when necessary. Here are some strategies for creating balance in your life:

- ☐ Identify your priorities: Take some time to think about what's most important to you in life. What are your values? What brings you joy? Once you have a clear understanding of your priorities, it will be easier to make decisions that align with them.

- ☐ Set boundaries: Create clear boundaries between work and play, productivity and relaxation, and anything else that requires balance in your life. Stick to these boundaries as much as possible, and be willing to say no when necessary.

- ☐ Practice self-care: Make time for self-care activities that help you recharge and feel your best. This could be anything from getting enough sleep to exercising regularly, or practicing meditation or mindfulness.

- ☐ Learn to delegate: If you're feeling overwhelmed, learn to delegate tasks to others. This could mean asking a colleague to take on some of your work, or asking a friend or family member to help with household chores.

- ☐ Stay flexible: Remember that life is unpredictable, and there will be times when you need to adjust your plans. Be willing to adapt and make changes as necessary, while still prioritizing balance and harmony in your life.

# CHAPTER 9: MANAGING STRESS AND CULTIVATING RESILIENCE

Life is full of challenges and unexpected events that can cause stress and take a toll on our physical and mental well-being. Stress, if not managed effectively, can lead to a variety of health problems, including anxiety, depression, and chronic illness. In this chapter, we will discuss strategies for managing stress and building resilience to cope with life's challenges.

# THE IMPACT OF STRESS ON OUR PHYSICAL AND MENTAL HEALTH

Stress is a normal part of life, and in some cases, it can be helpful in motivating us to take action. However, when stress becomes chronic or overwhelming, it can have a negative impact on our physical and mental health. Chronic stress can lead to high blood pressure, heart disease, weakened immune system, and increased risk of mental health issues such as anxiety and depression.

# STRATEGIES FOR MANAGING STRESS

There are several effective strategies for managing stress, and different techniques work better for different people. Here are a few strategies to consider:

- ☐ Mindfulness: Mindfulness is a technique that involves being present in the moment and paying attention to your thoughts and feelings without judgment. Practicing mindfulness can help reduce stress and increase feelings of calm and well-being.
- ☐ Exercise: Regular exercise has been shown to reduce stress and improve mood. Exercise can also help you sleep better, which can further reduce stress.
- ☐ Self-Care: Taking care of yourself is crucial for managing stress. Make time for activities that you enjoy and that help you relax, such as reading, taking a bath, or spending time in nature.

# BUILDING RESILIENCE

Resilience refers to our ability to bounce back from challenges and adversity. Building resilience can help us cope with stress and overcome setbacks. Here are some techniques for building resilience:

- ☐ Cultivate a positive mindset: Practice gratitude and focus on the good things in your life. This can help shift your perspective and increase feelings of optimism and resilience.
- ☐ Learn from challenges: When faced with challenges, reflect on what you learned and how you can apply that knowledge to future situations.
- ☐ Build a support system: Having a supportive network of friends and family can help you through difficult times and increase resilience.

# REDUCING STRESS
# IN DAILY LIFE

In addition to managing stress and building resilience, there are several techniques you can use to reduce stress in your daily life:

- ☐ Simplify your life: Identify the things that are causing stress and see if there are ways to simplify or reduce those stressors.
- ☐ Practice self-compassion: Be kind to yourself and avoid self-criticism.
- ☐ Set boundaries: Learn to say no to commitments that don't align with your priorities and values.

# CHAPTER 10: FINAL THOUGHTS

Now that you have learned how to design your life, it's important to remember that the journey towards a well-lived, joyful life is ongoing. As you grow and change, so will your goals and priorities. Continue to assess your values and create an action plan that aligns with them.

Remember to celebrate your successes, no matter how small, and be kind to yourself when setbacks occur. Cultivate a supportive environment and surround yourself with people who inspire and motivate you.

Always make time for your passions and purpose, and use them to make a positive impact on the world. And most importantly, remember to live a balanced life that includes both work and play, productivity and relaxation.

Designing your life is a process that takes time, effort, and patience. It requires self-reflection, goal-setting, and the willingness to make changes and take risks. But the result is a life that is well-lived, fulfilling, and joyful.

By assessing your values, defining your ideal life, cultivating healthy habits, creating a supportive environment, navigating challenges, cultivating meaningful relationships, pursuing your passions and purpose, and living a balanced life, you can design a life that brings you true happiness.

So take the time to design your life, and remember that the

journey is just as important as the destination.